WHAT YOU SHOULD KNOW ABOUT

LIVING

WITH

ONE PARENT

WHAT YOU SHOULD KNOW ABOUT

LIVING

WITH

ONE PARENT

WILLIAM L. COLEMAN

WHAT YOU SHOULD KNOW ABOUT LIVING WITH ONE PARENT

Cover design: Bob Fuller
Interior design: Jim Brisson

Library of Congress Cataloging-in-Publication Data
Coleman, William L.
    What you should know about living with one parent / William L. Coleman.
        p. cm.
    ISBN 0-8066-2636-4 :
    1. Children of single parents—United States—Juvenile literature.
2. Single-parent family—United States—Juvenile literature.
3. Parent and child—United States—Juvenile literature. 4. Family—United States—Religious life—Juvenile literature. I. Title.
II. Title: Living with one parent.
HQ777.4.C65   1993
306.85′6—dc20   93-31851
                                                                CIP
                                                                AC

The paper used in this publication meets the minimum requirements of American National Standard for Information Sciences—Permanence of Paper for Printed Library Materials, ANSI Z329.48-1984.

Manufactured in the U.S.A.   AF 9-2636

97 96 95 94 93   1   2   3   4   5   6   7   8   9   10

◆ ◆ ◆ ◆ ◆

CONTENTS

5

◆ ◆ ◆ ◆ ◆

Suggestions for Adults

A child living with one parent has many issues to figure out. He or she can't be left to guess what is going on because frequently the guess will be wrong. That's why a child needs a caring adult like yourself to help explain the situation.

Millions of children will adjust well to a one-parent home if they have adequate information and a healthy sense of love. The enemies of children are ignorance and the lack of love. Every child should experience a caring relationship. If you can help supply that care for even one child, you do the work of God.

Single-parent families are not better or worse than those with two parents. There are too many variables. Life isn't that simple. Many two-parent families are unbearable war zones. One loving parent will always be better than two hateful parents.

The goal of this book is to supply some information and be a springboard for discussion. It should help children and adults to engage in valuable conversation. The most important things a child will learn will come from the adults who know their situation.

Don't assume that you know the child's questions. Children are too sophisticated to be stereotyped. Children must be free to ask whatever they want. If, for some reason, the answer cannot be given, the child should be told that.

Sometimes children are bewildered. They don't understand their own emotions, and it is hoped that the chapters in this book will help them put into words what they previously have only felt. In some cases it raises issues that a particular child doesn't care about. Children come in all shades of personalities.

This book is designed either to be read to the child or for the child to read alone. If an adult can be involved to discuss the subjects, the process will probably be more fulfilling.

As you share with a child, here are some general guidelines you will want to keep in mind:

1. *Take your time going through the book.* A chapter or two a day may be plenty. When appropriate, go back and reread chapters that catch the child's interest.
2. *Don't assume you know how the child feels.* Single parenting presents many different feelings. Let the child talk and explain how he or she sees the situation.
3. *Let the child disagree or express anger.* He or she could have deep feelings of resentment and needs someone to listen. Don't let hostility frighten you. If you have serious concerns, be sure to contact

a clergy person, counselor, or other professional.

4. *Spend time with the child.* Even ten to fifteen minutes a day could prove life-changing.

5. *Raise any questions you think are important.* Sometimes children don't know how to express what it is they want to know. If the child says he or she doesn't have a problem with a certain subject, accept what the child says.

6. *Be truthful.* Never lie to a child. Once you destroy the trust factor, you may no longer be able to help him or her. If you can't answer a question or would rather not answer it, say so, but do not lie.

7. *Try not to defend or attack a parent.* Don't get in the middle, but if there are certain facts the child must know for purposes of safety, share those facts.

8. *Consistently remind the child of God's love.* Family relationships are so confusing that children should be assured that no matter what changes in their lives, God loves them always.

9. *Your personal attention is one of the most valuable contributions you can make.* Caring for a child is close to the heart of God. Jesus draws them near and lets them know how special they are.

◆ ◆ ◆ ◆ ◆

Each Family Is Different

No two families are exactly the same. Like fingerprints, we each have a unique family. Dads are different; mothers are different; children come in different sizes, hair color, and number of freckles. Most families do not have a pet tiger but some do.

Your family has its own characteristics, favorite meals, and its own funny stories to tell. One chief feature of your family is that you only have one parent. That doesn't make you good or bad. It's just a fact.

For years there was only one parent in the family where I grew up. Sometimes that was hard but what I remember most was how good it was. I hope that's what you will remember, too.

God bless you and your single-parent family.

Bill Coleman

♦ ♦ ♦ ♦ ♦

You Got a Dirty Deal

Absolutely! Let's admit that right away. It would have been terrific if you had two parents living together and loving each other. That's the way it was meant to be, but something happened and it didn't quite work out that way.

In the future you might get a stepparent, or maybe your absent parent might return. But today you have a dirty deal. None of us has a perfect life. Not having a parent may be painful for you, but every person carries some kind of problem. Everyone hurts because of bad experiences that affect them.

When you don't get everything, it's easy to feel sorry for yourself. You wonder why you couldn't have had a better or a fuller family. It hurts to see other families complete with father and mother all living together. Some days you sink into self-pity and think, "Poor me. I don't have everything."

All around us are families that aren't perfect. One family might have a relative who is an alcoholic. Another family has a member with a serious illness. A third family has a father out of work and there is a possibility that they might lose their home. Some families have all of those things happening at once.

We all have to learn to handle big disappointments. Not just little ones like dropping our dessert or missing a favorite television show. There are gigantic, painful setbacks. And they don't just happen to others; they happen to us, too.

There are many happy moments to live for: good people to meet and enjoy; beaches, forests, mountains, and valleys to run through and climb. There are bikes to ride, boats to sail, games to play, puzzles to solve, and jobs to do. If you sit and feel sorry for yourself, you will miss too many good things. If you live in anger or hate, if you concentrate on losses and disappointments, all the happiness will pass you by.

No matter how much of a "dirty deal" you think you have received, there will always remain some good news. That good news is that God will stay with you forever: in the bad times and when your heart aches, during the good times when you sing from the inside out. Through every circumstance and every event, your Heavenly Father will never go away. God's love for us is a good deal. We can never lose God's closeness and love. "Never will I leave you; never will I forsake you" (Hebrews 13:5).

◆ ◆ ◆ ◆ ◆

Why Is Your Parent Single?

Many millions of children will spend some time living with one parent. It could be for six months, or two years, or possibly all of their lives. You probably know several children in school or at church who live with just one parent. Perhaps some adults you know grew up with one parent for a while.

Living with one parent is different than living with two parents, but it's very common. Some of the happiest children you know may have only one parent. I lived with one parent for about four years and some of my best memories are of that time.

Often when a parent is single we guess that he must be divorced. That's probably the biggest reason why parents don't have partners. But it's not the only reason. Look at some of the major causes:

- divorced or separated
- death of a partner
- never married
- mental illness
- partner in prison
- partner away in military
- lengthy hospitalization
- partner missing

Maybe you can think of some other reasons why parents are single. These eight will cover most situations. Every young person should know why his or her parent is single. Children can guess or dream what the reason is, but they are better off if a parent explains the facts.

If you don't know why your parent is single, ask. Wait for a quiet time when you can talk about it, but definitely bring up the question. By understanding the facts you can relax and enjoy being with your single parent. Not knowing the truth could make you fearful and confused. It could even lead to nightmares or other problems.

Respect your parent's privacy. He may not want to tell you everything about his life. But he needs to share anything that affects your life. If he can't share, find a trusted adult who can listen while you talk about your feelings. This might be a neighbor or teacher.

In most families where there is one parent living at home, that parent is a mother. Only 5 to 10 percent of single parents are fathers, but either mothers or fathers can make excellent parents.

If you don't know or aren't sure why you have a single parent, be certain to ask your parent. You shouldn't have to wonder forever. If the answer isn't clear, ask your parent to explain it further. Ask questions. Don't feel silly or rude.

Having a single parent is a big part of your world. Knowledge of the facts will make your life easier to enjoy.

◆ ◆ ◆ ◆ ◆

Do You Worry About Your Parent?

When two people carry a large log, you don't worry about them. The right size log isn't too much for two healthy people to lift and move around.

But if you were to see one person carrying that same log, you might become concerned. One person alone could strain her back or drop the log. The one person could walk around the corner and bump into someone or knock the glass out of a car window.

It looks like one person carrying a log has a lot more to be careful about than if there were someone to help. Most of life seems to go easier if you have someone you can count on to lend a hand.

Some children have only one parent at their house, and they can see that parent has a lot of responsibility. They worry about that one parent. They wonder if their parent is working too hard, getting enough sleep, drinking too much, eating right, or if her job is too difficult.

Often young people won't say anything about their worries. They hold them inside and "fret." Sometimes worrying inside causes us to get sick. Children can feel stomach pains or burning; they can't sleep, don't want to eat, and can't study. A few children have lost hair from worrying.

Do you ever feel nervous or anxious or upset and you don't know why? You know something is bothering you but you can't explain what it is?

If you have worries that "hide inside," those fears could hurt you. It's important to bring them out and explain them to your parent. You can tell your parent that you worry about her health, job, finances, loneliness, boyfriend, temper—whatever.

Your parent needs to know what concerns you. Your parent shouldn't have to guess what is bothering you. You need to communicate. You need to say something like, "I'm afraid that you don't get enough sleep," or whatever it is.

When you express your worries in a kind and loving way, you are likely to get a good response from your parent. Some parents might become upset, but most will be glad to know that their child cares about them.

A parent might answer by saying, "Oh, don't worry about me." Don't let that brush you off. Tell her again that it does bother you. Your parent might be able to change if she realizes her behavior is worrying you.

If your parent can't or won't talk with you about these concerns, find another adult you trust. Your feelings are important.

Don't stop there. Also tell God what is worrying you. In a short prayer let God know how your parent's behavior makes you feel. Once you tell God, you will know that you're not in this alone. Ask God to help you carry this worry. It helps to know that another person—in this case God—will become involved and work on the problem with you. "Leave all your worries with him, because he cares for you" (1 Peter 5:7 TEV).

◆ ◆ ◆ ◆ ◆

You Can't Parent Your Parent

When you love others, usually you want to:

help them
protect them
care for them
be near them
solve their problems
and good things like that

It's great to feel very deeply about someone you love. Most people see what they can do to share with a person and try to meet his needs. That's what love does.

When you love a single parent, it is important to know that you can go too far in caring for him. Some children try to act like a parent to their single parent. They think they know what's best for their parent. They begin to tell their parent what to do.

Suppose you think your parent is taking too much medicine or alcohol.

Suppose you don't like your parent's friends.

Suppose you don't like his job.

Suppose you wish your parent would lose weight.

Suppose you think he should go out more.

When a parent and a child are very close, the child is tempted to try and run the parent's life. The child feels responsible for the parent's actions and can become burdened about his parent.

Parents are adults and need to be responsible for their own decisions. Back off and let your parent run his own life. If your parent's actions are somehow hurting you, then you need to tell him or another trusted adult. Otherwise, you need to respect your parent and trust his decisions.

Be careful that you don't get turned upside down. When children become parents and parents become children, you could end up being your own grandparent! There are enough problems without everyone getting topsy-turvy.

Sometimes parents need to make decisions for their children, but children shouldn't have to make decisions for their parents. Single parents need many things from their children. They need cooperation, obedience, love, respect, helpfulness, and a great deal more. Relax. They don't need their children to parent them.

◆ ◆ ◆ ◆ ◆

The Courage of a Single Parent

Usually we use the word *courage* to describe soldiers. If they have fought a dangerous battle, we think of them as tough and brave. We also use the word *courage* when talking about rescue workers. Someone who brings a lost child out of a dark cave shows the courage to take risks.

In many families, single parents are just as courageous. They aren't sure how to raise children by themselves. A single parent may wonder about many things: Should I try to be both mother and father at the same time? How can I provide all the things my child needs? Will I be able to answer the questions children ask? What if my child gets sick? Where can I go to for help?

Single parents still hang in there. Some very good parents have had to give up their children for adoption. That can be a courageous thing to do, too. But your parent has chosen to make a home for you, and you need one another.

When your parent is tired and grouchy or short-tempered, it would be easy to get angry at her. But remember, she has chosen a difficult route to travel. It would be hard for her to be upbeat every day, just like it's hard for you to be cheerful all the time.

God has given you a special person in your life: a courageous single parent. When the going gets rough, remind yourself how brave and caring she is.

◆ ◆ ◆ ◆ ◆

Single Fathers

Two kinds of children live with a single father. Some live with him for short visits, like weekends or vacations. They live with their mother most of the year but spend some time with Dad. This describes the relationship many children have with their single fathers.

The second kind is when children live for most of the year with a single father. There aren't as many families like this, but there are still quite a few.

If you live with a single father, he probably has custody. He is primarily responsible for taking care of you.

I can't think of anything that a father can't take care of for a child. Fathers can cook and wash and braid hair. They can give baths, go to PTA meetings, play catch, and take children to the bathroom at 2:00 in the morning.

Like many mothers, many fathers communicate extremely well with their children. Like mothers, fathers can be a lot of fun. They can take you places, go on rides, go to church, go camping, and eat pizza.

When children get sick, a dad might have trouble getting off work to take them to the doctor, but it can be done. Some fathers have to educate their bosses, but that can happen. Fathers enjoy their children. They can get involved and be close to their children. Often a single father will work extra hard at getting to know his children. Single fathers want and need to get close to the children, and that's good for everyone.

If a child doesn't have a mother present, that child loses a great deal. Mothers are not only important but also terrific, but so are fathers. There are many good points in living with a father.

Look at the fingers on one of your hands. Count five good reasons why you like living with Dad. That's simply the beginning. Begin to enjoy those five reasons and before long you might be able to count five more on the second hand, too.

Living with a single father is rare, but it can be exciting.

◆ ◆ ◆ ◆ ◆

Absent Parents

If you are living with one parent, how do you feel about your other parent? Maybe you see that parent once in a while—possibly never. Some children have never met their other parent.

When you think about the other parent, what do you think? Are you angry? Are you bewildered and confused? Do you ever dream that you are with him or her? Do you get sad, or happy, or cheerful, or blue thinking about your missing or absent parent?

Some children have met their missing parent and haven't enjoyed the meeting. At first they had very little to talk about or do together and felt awkward with each other. Many have found their missing parent fascinating and want to spend more time together.

Why not tell the parent you live with how you feel about the parent you don't live with? Explain how you think about that person. Have you ever met him? Do you wish you could? Do you want to know why your parents aren't living together or maybe aren't married? These are important questions. You deserve some kind of answer; after all, these are your parents.

Would you like to see your absent parent more often? Less often? Why do you feel that way? You might not know exactly how you feel but if you try to explain it to someone, your feelings might become clearer to you.

Exactly why two parents don't live together is a problem between two parents. In a way, that's their business, but their decision to not live together affects the children. Therefore children have a right to know something about the reason.

The reason why a parent is absent could be a tough puzzle. Maybe the absent parent doesn't want to come around. Maybe he can't come around. Maybe the parent you live with doesn't want the other parent to come around. Maybe no one knows where the other parent is. There are so many possibilities that you might never guess the correct answer.

It's better to ask and get more information.

Sometimes parents think their children know exactly what is going on when they don't. Later they will say, "Oh, I thought you knew about that." All the time the children were in the dark about what was happening.

If you don't know why one of your parents is absent, you might start to fantasize. You may wonder, "Is my parent far away on a ship? Is he homeless or rich and living on an estate? Does he have an important job and have to be in Asia six months each year?

You should not have to fill in the blanks. It isn't fair. Ask your parent where your absent parent is. If your parent is uncomfortable talking about it, you might try a relative or another trusted adult. You deserve an honest answer.

♦ ♦ ♦ ♦ ♦

Never-Married Mothers

All of us have fathers, even if they aren't married to our mothers. Millions of children live with never-married mothers. A never-married mother could mean many things for your family. How many of the following are true of your mother?

- She is less likely to get financial help from your father.
- She probably doesn't get emotional support or encouragement from your father. (Often, her parents and other relatives do help out.)
- She has to make decisions about her children without another parent to talk to. (That's scary for some mothers.)
- Her decision to keep you may have been a difficult one.
- Some days she may doubt if she is strong enough to do everything that is needed.
- She has a deep commitment to care for you.

These things may not be equally true in your situation. If you discuss them with your mother, you might receive a good idea of how she sees you and loves you.

The most famous mother in the world is probably Mary, the mother of Jesus. Jesus was conceived in her womb by God. Joseph was not the biological father.

For a while Joseph wondered whether or not to marry Mary, who was already pregnant. Finally, he decided to marry the woman he loved and act as the father of her child.

Mary came very close to being a never-married mother. If that had been the case Jesus would have had a family like the millions of others we have mentioned. She would have understood the difficulties of raising a child alone. No doubt Mary would have found the strength to be a single parent if she had needed it.

God would have loved Mary and Jesus even if Joseph had decided not to marry her. Our heavenly Father loves never-married mothers as much as he loves all people. God sent Jesus Christ to die for everyone, including every mother. "For God so loved the world that he gave his one and only Son, that whoever believes in him shall not perish but have eternal life" (John 3:16).

◆ ◆ ◆ ◆ ◆

God, Our Heavenly Parent

What is a family? We used to think it was a mother, a father, three children, a dog, a cat, and maybe a gerbil. Of course that is a family, but it isn't the only kind. Families come in all sizes and varieties.

A family can have one parent, twelve children, and a pet turtle. Families can have a grandparent or two, a stepbrother, and a bowl of tropical fish. Many families change. A child may live with relatives or a foster family for a time and then live somewhere else. Maybe the single parent will marry, adding a stepparent and three other children.

Families aren't made up of only a certain number of people. They don't have to include a brother, or a dog, or a van. They don't even have to all use the same last name.

Usually a family is a group of people that lives together, and hopefully they are committed to care for each other. The children may not be legally adopted or they may be stepsisters, but they are in a family relationship and they pull together much of the time.

God is our parent and God has a peculiar family. It consists of people of all ages and races and nationalities. They have come into the family through Jesus Christ. God's family members are short, tall, thin, and fat. They are quiet, noisy, bright, and not so bright.

Sometimes God acts like a father. "I will be a Father to you, and you will be my sons and daughters" (2 Corinthians 6:18). At other times God is described doing the work of a mother. "How often I have longed to gather your children together as a hen gathers her brood under her wings" (Matthew 23:37). That's the way most parents are: we do each other's jobs when we want to be helpful. God isn't a father or mother in the physical sense that we think of parents. But God is our heavenly parent. God loves us and wants the best for us.

Fortunately God understands all kinds of parenting. God sees loving grandparents raising their baby grandchild. God knows about the foster parents who open their homes to care for children. God understands parents who adopt children. God watches over the young mothers who raise their children alone. God also loves the mother who releases her child for adoption.

Every kind of family and every child is loved by God. God sees us pulling together and loving one another. This must make God glad!

"There is neither Jew nor Greek, slave nor free, male nor female, for you are all one in Christ Jesus. If you belong to Christ, then you are Abraham's seed, and heirs according to the promise" (Galatians 3:28-29).

◆ ◆ ◆ ◆ ◆

Other Adults

When there is only one parent living at your house, it could be important to have other adult friends. If your father doesn't live with you, you might want to get to know some other safe adult men; and if your mother doesn't live with you, other safe women friends could be helpful.

Naturally we aren't talking about just any adults. When you have adult friends, your parents should know who they are and they should approve of them. Don't keep friendships with adults unless your parent knows about it. Some adults aren't safe to be around.

There are several places where you could find good adult friends. First, there is your family. Grandparents, uncles, aunts, godparents, even older cousins may be able to do things for you and go places with you. Many people have great memories of their grandparents. They bake cookies, work on bikes, go to movies, take trips. Plus, grandparents are often good listeners.

If you belong to a club, a leader there may be willing to spend time with you. Girl Scouts, Boy Scouts, YWCA, Awana, karate clubs, youth groups, Sunday school classes—many of them have adult leaders who would make acceptable adult friends. Usually if they lead a group like this they enjoy children and are interested in them. Ask them whether they would be willing to spend time with you. Ask whether you can help them in any way. Make sure your parent knows them and you might find a good friendship.

School teachers and coaches are also busy but they often enjoy doing projects with young people. Join a team or volunteer to help after school. It's fun to be with children your own age, but time spent with a caring adult can help you feel more comfortable with adults.

Other adults can give children an outlet. If you don't feel like talking to your parent at a certain time, you might be able to share a problem with this other adult. All of us need a variety of people in our lives. A change of scenery and a change of people are much alike; they can make us feel better.

If you are going to spend time with another adult, tell your parent who it is. Your parents will probably be happy to agree; but if they don't approve, you need to accept that and not see the adult. When your grown friends are the right people, they can be a terrific help.

◆ ◆ ◆ ◆ ◆

Feel Like Crying?

Have you ever sat and thought about a second parent and wanted to cry? Don't be surprised if it hurts sometimes. Don't be disappointed if your heart aches. The loss of a parent is painful.

Even if the absent parent was harsh and abusive, it still hurts. You wish there could have been two healthy, happy parents living together. But right now you don't have two parents in your home. Sometimes you may wonder what it would be like to play in the park with a mother and a father. You might picture yourself on a roller coaster with Mom sitting on one side and Dad sitting on the other.

When you begin to think about your absent parent, do you ever feel tears filling up your eyes? Do you feel a lump in your throat and pain in your chest? Do you ever want to simply let go and cry?

If you feel like you are about to cry, let it go. Shedding tears may be exactly what you need to do. Holding back the tears could make you feel worse. A good hard cry every once in a while might be the best thing you can do at the time.

Sadness and stress build up inside. Tension makes you feel uptight, like a rubber band stretched too far. If you are able to cry, you can release some of that tension and "let it out."

We used to think that girls could cry but boys shouldn't. Today we know that it's all right for boys to cry, too. It's too hard if you cry only on the inside. When you feel sad you need to express that hurt. If you don't cry and release that sadness, it can turn into anger or depression. This can hurt you and others.

When you lose someone special, it is normal to feel that loss. It is as if you had an empty pocket inside of you. This absence makes you feel sad.

When Jesus lost a friend named Lazarus, he felt terribly sad. The Son of God loved his friend, Lazarus, and his sisters, Mary and Martha. Jesus was so moved by Lazarus's death that Jesus cried: "Jesus wept" (John 11:35).

The story of Jesus crying tells us several things: First, it's all right to cry when someone we love is gone. Second, it's all right for boys as well as girls to cry. Third, it's all right for adults to cry, too.

◆ ◆ ◆ ◆ ◆

Safety Net Calls

One of the most exciting acts at the circus is the tightrope walker. The acrobat must have a fantastic sense of balance to cross a wire with nothing to hold on to. Sometimes it looks like he is going to fall and go crashing to the ground.

You might see the walker carrying an umbrella. I saw one cross a wire with a person riding on his shoulders. Another time someone took a chair, placed it on the wire, and did a handstand on the chair.

It makes me feel better when tightrope walkers have a safety net under them. A few high wire performers have fallen and been killed. A safety net is a good idea.

You don't have to be a circus performer to need a safety net. All of us need people we can depend on in case we have trouble. What would you do if you fell down and broke a bone? Where would you call if you thought you were in danger? Where can you go if your single parent gets sick or doesn't come home on time? What if an adult is too rough with you or asks you to do something you are uncomfortable with? If you are lonely and sad, do you have a special person to call and talk to?

By now you probably have a list of telephone numbers of people to call for different reasons. Emergency numbers like the police or rescue squad are important. You should have your parent's work number. You should also have the number of a grandparent, or a special neighbor, or your other parent, or a counselor. These numbers should be posted by the phone or on the refrigerator or some place where they can be read easily.

Most days run smoothly but something unexpected might happen and you might need to get help in a hurry. Children aren't the only ones who need safety nets like this. Adults have lists of people they can call when they need help too.

Safety nets aren't just for emergencies. Sometimes we begin to feel uncomfortable, or nervous, or frightened, and we merely want to hear a friendly voice. After talking to them for a little while we usually calm down and feel better. We try not to stay on the phone too long in case someone tries to reach us in a hurry.

If you think of someone you want to add to the safety net list, put that person's number with the rest. Talk to your parent about others you might need to contact. It's smart to update the numbers once in a while.

When children abuse the phone by keeping it busy all day, parents are likely to get upset, but safety net calls are something else. Discuss those important calls with your parent.

37

◆ ◆ ◆ ◆ ◆

Talk, Don't Yell!

When Ashley felt frustrated, she used to raise her voice and scream. She thought that was the best way to get everyone's attention. Yelling will do that. Immediately Ashley's mother would turn around and scream back at her daughter. For two or three minutes the two would stand barking at each other like a couple of angry animals.

Because she yelled Ashley was able to get her mother's attention, get yelled back at, get everyone upset.

Every few days Ashley and her mother would yell at each other. Their screaming made their home a very unpleasant place to be. Some evenings neither one of them really wanted to go home.

To be truthful, sometimes shouting worked. Ashley would throw a fit and her mother would try to do what she wanted. And to be truthful, sometimes Ashley felt better because she could express what she needed to say.

But Ashley and her mother yelled and screamed too often. Their home sounded like the monkey house at the zoo. Not only was yelling noisy, but there was another problem. Soon both Ashley and her mother were saying some nasty things. They were beginning to call each other names and say things that they didn't mean. Screaming has a terrible way of getting out of control.

All of us need to communicate. We have to say how we feel and explain what we need. Sometimes we even get upset. But talking is a better way to explain things than yelling.

Lower the noise volume where you live! Shouting isn't the best way to communicate, and neither is pouting. Talking is an excellent way to express ourselves.

When you argue with someone, try to keep these important ideas in mind:

1. *Don't shout.* That usually makes other people shout, too. It is easier to think if the noise level is kept low.
2. *Don't call people names.* Insults get people upset and take us away from the real problem we need to solve.
3. *Explain the problem clearly.* Be specific. Describe the situation in one sentence and then discuss it further if necessary.
4. *Share solutions.* Ask the person how this problem could be solved. Explain how you think it could be corrected. Then try to reach an agreement.
5. *Reject the actions, not the person.* We can ask people to change their behavior and still like the people. Sometimes we have to avoid people because of their behavior, but not usually.

39

"A gentle answer turns away wrath, but a harsh word stirs up anger" (Proverbs 15:1).

Tell God About It

When you feel thankful for your parent and you know how much this person means to you, take time to tell God about it. God isn't just for complaints and requests. God wants to hear the good news too! If you think your parent is the greatest, be sure and let God know.

Do you ever wonder if your parent is overworked and stressed out? Ask God to make life a little easier for him. Maybe tomorrow will go better at work or a tough job may go smoother. Tell God that you are worried.

Have you felt uptight lately? Is there a lot of tension between you and your parent? When two or more people live close together, some tension is bound to build. Tell God that you want to calm down and become more loving and patient. Just talking to God about it has a way of unloading the burden.

How do you picture tomorrow? Do you hope for a different house or apartment? Do you need more food or clothing? God wants to help meet those needs too. Would you like to see someone's health improve? Would you like to meet new friends or find a good church?

God is interested in hearing from us and he likes to answer prayers. Tell God where you feel the gaps are in your life and ask God to help fill them. God loves each one of us and our families.

"But in everything, by prayer and petition, with thanksgiving, present your requests to God" (Philippians 4:6).

◆ ◆ ◆ ◆ ◆

Brain Battles

When you feel distant and tense about the parent you live with, you need to get closer. It's no fun being uptight. It's miserable avoiding each other and refusing to talk. Nobody enjoys living like this. It's like being at war in your minds. Mental fights wear us out and make us grouchy.

If two people are having brain battles, one of them has to make an effort to stop the war. But sometimes no one knows how to call a truce and end it. Who is going to make the first move toward peace?

Usually each person thinks, "He started the fight; let him end it." When both people feel that way, no one is going to make the first move. The longer the two are in the brain battle, the harder

41

it is to quit. Sometimes people fight for weeks and they can't remember how the war even started.

When you're tired of the fighting and you don't care who started it, there is a way to end the hostilities. If you will say one of these two things you will probably cool the war down or end it altogether.

Here is a suggestion. Either say: "Do you still give back rubs around here?" or "How would you like a back rub?"

Nothing works all the time, but these two sentences often help. Even if your parent says no, or just grunts, or says maybe later, at least you have broken the ice. Your parent knows you are willing to cut the tension a little bit.

Most of us can benefit a great deal from a good back rub. A back rub usually:

gets us closer
relaxes our tension
says we care
makes us feel accepted
makes us feel secure
makes us feel loved

when a back rub is given by a relative who really does care.

The problem with a back rub is, Who is going to suggest it? If two people sit around waiting for the other to ask for a back rub, spiders could build cobwebs in your hair before anything gets done.

Somebody needs to become the peacemaker. Someone has to make the first effort to call off the war.

God loves peacemakers. Peacemakers are brave people who take a chance and try to call off the brain battles. God will bless the lives of those who try to bring about peace with their parents or children.

"Blessed are the peacemakers, for they will be called children of God" (Matthew 5:9 NRSV).

◆ ◆ ◆ ◆ ◆

If You Had Your Way

Do you ever wish things were different? If you had your way, would money grow on trees? Would automobiles be free? Would video games come in boxes of breakfast cereal?

If you could wave a magic wand, would frogs turn into friends and grasshoppers into servants? What if you could simply say a secret word and potatoes would become ice cream, or broccoli would turn into pizza with pepperoni and cheese?

Imagine that you could merely wink and all of your schoolwork would be done. English would become easy and science would become clear. If you had your way, you could stay up half the night watching movies. Why not have dancing socks? You could throw them on the floor and they would run over to the dirty clothes pile all by themselves.

If you had your way you might make your family different. Parents might love each other forever if you had the power to make it happen. If you could, you would simply nod your head and relatives would stop arguing forever. You might snap your fingers and the yelling would stop or point your finger and the stress would be lifted.

God didn't give us the magic to make things our way. Too bad, it could have been fun. But God does give us the patience to accept what we cannot change. God gives us the love to care for people who are not perfect. God gives us the hope to help those who need us.

Families aren't always going to turn out our way. They probably aren't going to be God's way either. But a family can be special, exactly the way it is.

◆ ◆ ◆ ◆ ◆

Late Ball Practice

Gina sat by the front door with her glove in her hand. Nervously, she fidgeted with her baseball hat as she sat in the overstuffed chair. First she pushed the red hat high on her forehead, then she pulled it down tight, close to her ears. Next Gina took it off and half twirled the hat on her fingers.

Gina's mother had said she would pick her up at 10:00 A.M. to take her to practice. The VCR showed the time to be 10:15. Gina grew nervous and tried not to look at the flashing seconds that soon turned into minutes.

This didn't happen often. Her mother was busy but she tried hard to keep her promises. She had been late for a play once and Gina could still remember going backstage twelve minutes late. Gina didn't forget things like that.

She picked up a magazine and started flipping through the pages. "Think about something else," she told herself. "Look at the new jackets and shoes," she thought. The red digits on the VCR turned to 10:21. Gina threw the magazine at a vacant chair.

Gina pushed her lips together and then twisted them, the way she does when she is angry. Then she twisted them rapidly, which meant she was really mad.

45

Thump, thump. Footsteps could be heard on the stairs. Gina stood and opened the apartment door. There she saw a woman holding two grocery bags. Dirt and grease covered the woman's face and the front of her pink blouse. Despite the new rumpled look, Gina could tell it was her mother.

"I had a flat," her mother explained with a grin. "Please forgive me. I was hurrying as fast as I could."

Gina took one bag and started to chuckle.

"What's to forgive?" Gina laughed.

"Be kind and compassionate to one another, forgiving each other, just as in Christ God forgave you" (Ephesians 4:32).

◆ ◆ ◆ ◆ ◆

Send a Tape or Write a Letter

Is there someone you haven't seen for a long time but someone you would like to get in touch with? Maybe it's your other parent or a grandparent. Has a brother or a sister moved away? If that's your situation, the time may be right for you to make contact.

First, tell your parent what you have in mind. Whom do you want to contact? Your parent should be able to furnish you with the exact address. If not, ask if he would try and get it for you.

Sometimes if you haven't heard from a relative for such a long time you begin to wonder if he or she wants to keep in touch. Most relatives want to know how we are doing but they let things slide. It is important for us to make the first move. When everyone waits for the other person to do something, nothing gets done.

Once you have the address, ask yourself how to make this fun. If you have a tape recorder, you could have a good time recording your message. You could simply talk on the tape or you could add a little excitement by making sound effects or playing music in the background.

You could have your dog bark on the tape or even have a few words from a friend. Make the main message of the tape solid information about yourself: what you are doing; what your interests are; who your teachers are; what your church is like. Also include some feelings. Tell the person how much you care about him.

Ask a few questions and encourage the person to send back a tape. It means a lot to know that you want to hear from him.

The tape doesn't have to be long. A short message and the sound of your voice will be appreciated by the listener.

If you don't have a tape recorder or don't like speaking on a tape, a letter or a picture will do just fine. The important thing is to get in touch with someone you care about. Letters don't have to be long either. A couple of paragraphs on one side of a page will say that you care.

When you want to hear from someone special, the best thing to do is take the first step. They will probably be excited to hear from you.

◆ ◆ ◆ ◆ ◆

People Who Brood

Brooding is an old-fashioned word. After a chicken lays an egg, the mother hen sits on that egg to keep it warm. If the mother sits for a long time the egg might hatch open and give life to a new baby chick. This is called brooding.

There isn't a great deal of activity to brooding. The better the hen sits still on the egg, the sooner it is likely to hatch.

When people sit around worrying, that is also called brooding. We aren't sitting on eggs, but we do stay in one place. While we are in that one spot we think, and speculate, and ponder, and fret, and wonder what will happen next.

We might lie on the bed or sit in a chair. We cross our legs, scratch our heads, fold our arms, unfold them, and then fold them again. Usually we have a stern look and often our forehead will wrinkle as we frown.

That look means we think we have a serious problem and we need to give it some deep thought. But if we think about our problems all of the time, we have started to brood. Thinking over a problem can help us solve that difficulty. Mulling over it for hour after hour can turn into useless brooding.

There is no special age for brooders. Adults frequently do it. Do you ever see your parent sitting alone with that spaced-out look? Her eyes look straight ahead, but they aren't really seeing anything. Most likely they are brooding over something.

Some people think children don't brood. They say that children don't have serious problems, so why would they brood? But children realize that sometimes they have lots to worry about. Brooding is common among children. Sometimes they can't figure out what is happening in their families and they get frustrated trying to understand it all. That's when some children begin to brood.

There is a big difference between thinking and brooding. Thinking is trying to find an answer to a problem. But brooding means we sit too long and worry too much. Brooding makes us feel bad and very seldom do we solve problems by sitting around for hours. Brooding adds to our difficulties.

If you find yourself brooding or sitting too long, you need to do something to change that. You need to get up, move around, and become active. Simply say to yourself, "I refuse to brood," and stand up. Then move.

Take a walk. Play a game. Find a friend. Cook pizza. The best solution for brooding is to get moving. Start thinking about something else.

It's all right for a mother hen to brood, but if you aren't hatching eggs, you need to get up and start moving!

What's Good About It?

To hear some people talk, you would think that having one parent is the worst thing that ever could have happened to them. Having a single parent does have its difficulties. But you and I know that there are some advantages to living with one parent. If you look closely, you will find some good points.

Are any of these things true in your family?

- You get extra attention from a single parent.
- You get to try more things like cooking and fixing things yourself and taking responsibility.

- You get to make more choices like where to go, and what to eat, and which movie to watch.
- You become more a part of an adult world because you are included in what your parent does. Sometimes that's cool.

Did you find that a couple of those describe your situation? You probably won't agree with all four. Look at this second list and see if these are true in your home.

- You feel needed. Everyone pulls together and you know you are important to your family.
- You are drawn close to the one parent. Some single parents show their happy side as well as their sad side when they spend more time with their children.
- Is there less fighting? Sometimes living with one parent means there is less tension. When your parents aren't yelling, you can feel more relaxed.
- There is less arguing about the children. Often two parents disagree over what the children are and are not allowed to do.

How many of those four things are true at your house? Do they make you think of other good things?

Take a piece of paper and write down a few of the good things about living with one parent.

Your list may be entirely different than the eight I have written. Think it over and be positive.

Having one parent can be very hard. We know that. But the Bible teaches us to look for the good things. There are almost always good things if we search for them.

"Finally, brothers, whatever is true, whatever is noble, whatever is right, whatever is pure, whatever is lovely, whatever is admirable—if anything is excellent or praiseworthy—think about such things" (Philippians 4:8).

◆ ◆ ◆ ◆ ◆

Find a Good Group

Would you like to meet once a month with people your age who live with one parent? Would you like to get together to have fun and discuss what life is like with a single parent? It might be a great way to meet new friends and learn at the same time.

Maybe you would like to ask other children how they handle tough subjects like meeting their mothers' or fathers' dates or baby-sitting brothers and sisters. What do other children do when their father or mother forgets to call? The group may also have an experienced adult who could make helpful suggestions.

If a group sounds like a good idea, tell your parent. They may be able to help you find one that is right for you.

There are a couple of places you could begin looking for a group like this. The first place might be your local church. Call the church office and ask if such a group exists. If the answer is no, say that you would like to be part of one if the church starts a group. You probably have some friends with one parent; tell the church about them, too.

It wouldn't be a strange idea for a church to start such a group. Many single parents attend church. One out of three adults in the church I attend is divorced. Your church may have more. The church leaders may never have thought of helping the children of single parents.

If for any reason that doesn't work, there are organizations that can help you. One of them is called Parents without Partners. Look in your phone book for the number. There may be such a group near you.

I used to think that groups were silly. But groups can be helpful. They allow people the chance to share how they feel and what they have learned. Groups are good places to find out that other people feel many of the same things you do.

Discuss it with your parent. A group could be good for both of you.

♦ ♦ ♦ ♦ ♦

Feeling Afraid

Most of us are afraid of something. Noises in the night, horror stories, scary music, big dogs, creepy people who stand on street corners. Adults are afraid just as much as children. Sometimes adults are afraid of the same things as children.

Change is one of the things that scares us the most. We are afraid of a new teacher, a new neighborhood, a new set of friends. When a situation changes we are afraid of how we will handle something that's different.

If a mother gets a new boyfriend or a new husband, or a father gets a new girlfriend or a wife, that might scare a child, at least for a while. New brothers or sisters could be just as scary at first. Sometimes we become afraid of things that no one else knows about. We might be afraid of a new baby-sitter, mother's new working hours, someone who moves in a few houses away.

It isn't silly to feel afraid. Usually if you are afraid, there is a reason for the fear. If you tell your parent about your fear, he or she can probably help you with it. Your parent can answer questions, or fix something so it won't be noisy, or explain what is really going on, or suggest ways to avoid problems. Children often feel better after they describe their fears to their parents.

If you would rather not talk to your parent, find another adult you trust, like a pastor or school counselor.

The fears that hurt the most are the ones we hide inside. We don't want to talk about them. We think people won't understand or will make fun of us. Some boys even believe they can't be a man if they admit they are afraid. When we keep our fear inside we make ourselves miserable and we have trouble getting rid of the fear.

It's hard to be afraid and be happy at the same time. Imagine that you had a large fishbowl with thirty little fish called Happiness. In that same bowl there was a big, grouchy fish called Fear. Pretend that every day the Fear fish ate a couple of the Happiness fish. You know you have to remove the Fear fish or soon there won't be any Happiness fish left.

Tell your parent or another trusted adult about the fear before it eats up all your happiness.

Sometimes you feel afraid and you don't know what about. It's all right to tell your parent that, too. Your parent might be able to help you understand what makes you afraid.

◆ ◆ ◆ ◆ ◆

Are Single-Parent Kids Trouble?

If there is only one parent living at your house, are you going to grow up to be a maladjusted, nasty troublemaker? Will you push old people down or steal ice cream from little kids on the street corner? Will you be arrested for window peeping or run off with the neighbor's parrot? Will you get pregnant, or make someone else pregnant, or sniff drugs until your eyes pop out?

Those are the kinds of questions some people ask about the children of single parents. Are they growing up to become the enemies of society because they don't have two parents under one roof?

The answer to this question is simple. A child with one parent at home can decide if he wants to be a levelheaded kid or a troublemaker. That's his decision to make. It is the same decision that children with two parents at home need to make.

A person's background, nationality, race, neighborhood, family life—these cannot make us good or bad. We behave according to decisions we finally make ourselves. A loving, caring, one-parent family can be a terrific environment!

People who say, "Children from single-parent families are just trouble" don't know what they are talking about. They are showing their prejudice. They are judging someone they don't even know. Children come in all sizes and varieties. Sometimes children with good behavior come from terrible families and children with bad behavior come from almost perfect families.

It isn't cause and effect. Single parent families don't cause children to go bonkers. We all have choices to make about who we want to be and how we want to act.

Sometimes children are confused by what they read in the newspaper or hear on television. They hear discussions about broken families or children in trouble with the police. Life can be hard and living with one parent can be difficult, but children usually are able to make up their minds about which way they want to go.

Some of the best parents in the world are single parents.

Some of the finest children alive grew up with one parent.

By the grace of God, each of us has the power to be the kind of person we choose to become.

People to Pray For

Every family could use some prayer—no matter if the family is going through change every day or if they merely sit around each evening watching reruns of Zoo Parade. Dull families, exciting families, calm families, explosive families, noisy families, and motorcycle families all need prayer.

If you would like to pray for your family, where do you start? A good place to begin is by praying for yourself. Some of us are too modest and we don't like to pray for ourselves. We don't like to talk about ourselves, and we think God must have more important things to do.

But praying for yourself may be your best prayer. You can ask God to change you, to give you wisdom, to give you courage, to help you understand. God can change your attitudes, show you how to forgive, and teach you patience. Just the act of talking to God begins to make us different right away.

Prayer means you have sought out someone else to talk to. It means you have shared your problems and asked for help. The few minutes you spend talking to God allows you to relieve tension and get your feelings out.

God is more than just someone to talk to. God is a good listener, but God can also make things happen. God can teach us to be loving, caring, and forgiving.

We also want to pray for parents, brothers, sisters, grandparents, and maybe others. But the first person we can pray for is ourselves.

Answer me when I pray,
O God, my defender!
When I was in trouble, you helped me.
Be kind to me now and hear my prayer
(Psalm 4:1 TEV).

Meeting Your Other Parent

Let's pretend that you have been living with one parent for as long as you can remember. There has always been only a single parent in your life. But you know it takes two people to make a child.

Who is your other parent?
Where is your other parent?
Would you like to meet your other parent?

Sooner or later you will probably become very curious about your missing or absent parent. Most children wonder a lot about who the parent is and what she is like.

It's possible that you can't meet your other parent.

- Your parent may have died.
- Your parent might live in another country that you cannot visit.
- Some mothers don't know who the father is. Maybe she spent a weekend with a man and has never seen him again.
- Sometimes a parent refuses to see his or her child.
- Your parent may have moved away and left no address.

There are many reasons why children never meet one of their parents. Some children have never met either of their natural parents.

When you want to meet your other parent, tell that to the parent you live with. This shouldn't be the question no one discusses. Your parent could give you the best answer possible. He may even be able to arrange a meeting for you in a short time.

Whatever happens, you need to talk about the parent who doesn't live with you. You need to know the facts and, if possible, you may enjoy meeting your other parent.

Your Parent's Feelings

Whenever Janie mentioned her father, she noticed that her mother would change the subject. Janie would say, "I got a letter from Dad today." Her mother would say, "I've got pizza baking in the oven." If Janie said, "Did you know Dad switched jobs?" her mother would say, "How would you like to go shopping this weekend?"

Janie's mother never seemed able or willing to talk about Dad. It puzzled her. She wondered why her mother couldn't at least forgive him for whatever he did and be nice to him. Janie felt good about both her mother and her father.

It's hard to say exactly why Janie's mother doesn't like to talk about Janie's father. Janie's mother has had experiences with her father that Janie probably doesn't know about. Her parents may have said things to each other and even done things to each other that were extremely painful.

If her mother feels badly toward her father, it's easy to see why she doesn't like to talk about him. She doesn't want to say terrible things about him in front of Janie. That would be "running him down" and she doesn't want to do that. And yet, Mother doesn't want to say much good about him either.

That's like having your tongue tied up. It can't say anything good and it can't say anything bad, so it doesn't say anything about him at all.

Mothers and fathers have to work out their own feelings. Children can't tell adults how to feel. But children can try to understand a little about their parents' feelings.

If a parent doesn't say anything about the other parent it could mean the parent is:

angry
protecting you
confused
sad
frustrated
or upset

Your parent could have a lot of other feelings too. She may not feel ready to express any thoughts. Sometimes your parent's answers, or replies, or silence may seem odd to you. Your parent also may have trouble understanding it.

Be patient with your parent. She is going through change, too.

Pretending

Not every night, but every now and then, David liked to pretend. He would lie on his bed in the dark and make up an ideal family. In his mind the pretend family would be almost perfect.

David imagined a father coming home every day. He would drive up in a shiny red car. As he walked toward the house, David could see something in his arms and he wondered if it was a present for him.

David could picture his mother and father sitting on the living room couch, talking playfully. His family would have a brother and a sister. Naturally they would be pests, but not too bad. David could see a dog and a cat lying on the floor or else playing with his brother.

In his mind, David could see the ideal family and he often wished it were his.

No one can blame David for dreaming. The problem is that there aren't many ideal families. No matter how many members we have or who they are, each of us has tough times. Some families with two parents at home don't get along at all. They argue and have financial problems and sometimes don't talk to each other, just like families with one parent.

Many children wish they had another family. Sometimes they wish their father were the football coach or the school principal. They might want a woman on television to be their mother. Children don't usually say that out loud but sometimes they wish it.

That doesn't mean they don't love their parents. They like to pretend. All of us pretend in some way, especially when times seem hard or tough.

But when we aren't pretending, most of us know the truth. Many children have only one parent and that parent loves them a great deal. One parent who loves you is worth far more than two parents who don't.

More important than how many parents we have is the question of love. Some children have two parents who love them and that's fantastic. Others have only one parent and that parent loves them. That's fantastic, too.

Pretending isn't bad, but sometimes reality isn't bad either. If we have one parent who loves us, we ought to be extremely thankful.

"And now these three remain: faith, hope and love. But the greatest of these is love" (1 Corinthians 13:13).

Ask Questions

Do you ever wonder where the stars go in the daytime? Do you know why you don't stop breathing when you go to sleep at night? Do horses sleep standing up or lying down? Do they ever roll over on their backs and sleep with their feet straight up in the air?

Life is full of a zillion questions:

Can penguins fly?
Can a person lift a car?
Can a fish close its eyes?

That's part of what makes life so amazing. There is always some new thing to investigate or learn about or to discover. A busy brain keeps looking around.

If you drop a rubber ball and a steel ball, which will bounce the highest? Which weighs more—a pound of feathers or a pound of mud? Can a parrot really talk?

Questions are good. By asking questions, we are likely to find answers.

Many children have questions about their families.

Who are your grandparents?
Where did your mother go to school?

What is your father's favorite food?
Does your mother enjoy being single?

We don't have to know everything about everybody, but some questions are important. Parents don't have to answer all of our questions, but at least we can ask.

What does mother do at her job?
Does mother have a "special" friend?
What is your father's favorite sport?
Where do your cousins live?
What is your father's favorite color?
Is your mother ever lonely?

These may not be the questions you want to ask. You should ask whatever questions you have. If your parent doesn't want to answer a question, he can say so. Maybe your parent can tell you why. Maybe he will answer it later.

Respect your parents and don't be pushy if they don't want to answer, but at least ask and find out. In some cases, your parent might be happy to answer but had no idea you wanted to know.

◆ ◆ ◆ ◆ ◆

Your Parent Needs Friends Too

Parents can't spend all their time with their children. That probably wouldn't be good for the children. It definitely wouldn't be best for the parents!

Adults need to spend time with adults sometimes, just like children need to be with children. Adults and children like to be with each other too, but not every minute. Most children don't want to attend lectures or concerts too often. Likewise, most adults can't play video games or ride bikes as long as children can.

Children and adults can mix well but not every hour of the day and night.

When parents sometimes want to do things with adults, their children should be glad. That means the parent is enjoying a full, well-rounded life. And it doesn't have to be a date. A parent can have both male and female friends.

You don't want your parent out every night or gone most of the time, but some children become frightened and want their parent around all of the time. If your parent comes home after work and just sits in the living room every evening, she could become a dull person. Your parent needs to get out.

The next time your parent wants to go bowling, or to a concert, or to a small group, or some place else with friends, be happy for her. When a parent is happy, a child is more likely to be happy too!

Is Your Parent Dating?

It can be lonely to be a single parent. He may enjoy being with his children, but he also needs an adult companion. Don't be surprised if your father finds someone to spend time with or to date. He may even date a number of people.

You may have thought dating was something for teenagers and college students. You probably never imagined your parent "dating." Some children are even embarrassed to think of their "old" parent going out on dates.

If you want to understand dating, you have to try and understand your parent's situation. Parents like to have friends just like children have friends. They need someone to talk to and someone to spend time with. Parents also need other adults who care about them. Life is so much easier when others care about us.

Certainly you and your parent care about each other, but most of us need more than that.

We want someone our age who is interested in us.

Most parents eventually find a special adult to share their life with. If the children will expect that and accept the new friend, everyone will probably be much happier.

When your parent starts to "date" or "see someone," that new person will have some effect on you. The new person will take up some of your parent's time. If she doesn't hang around the house, your parent's friend will at least come and go, say hello, ask about school, and things like that.

Try to remember how important dates are for your parent. You wouldn't want to lock your parent in the house and have him sit in a corner. Your parent's dates may make you feel uncomfortable at first but you can get used to them. Think of your parent. You want your mother or father to be happy, and this person could help make life more fun for your parent, and for you.

Do your best to meet the dates your parent brings home. It isn't that you will approve or disapprove of the date. Your parent is the parent. You are the child. It's not your job to inspect dates. You can't ground your parent. But it is friendly to meet your parent's companions and be on speaking terms with them. This is especially true if the dates keep coming regularly.

Dates aren't in competition with children. It would be easy to think that the date is stealing your parent's time and attention from you. If dating is done correctly there will still be plenty of time for your parent to have a good relationship with you.

If you are concerned about your parent's dates, tell your parent what is bothering you. Are you afraid of losing your parent? Are you being selfish? Does something about the new person concern or frighten you? Would you like to get to know the person better? Does your parent stay out too late and does that frighten you? If you can't talk with your parent, talk with another trusted adult.

The best thing to do with date questions is to ask them. The more you understand, the better you will feel and the closer you will be with your parent.

◆ ◆ ◆ ◆ ◆

Melanie Became a Monster

Usually Melanie was a terrific girl. She was great at helping around the house. Melanie liked to bake, made a delicious lasagna, and cared for her cat, Lukas. And when it came to obedience, Melanie was a B + . No angel, but this fifth grader was pretty cool to live with.

That is, until her 35-year-old mother started bringing dates to the house. Parent dates seemed to turn Melanie into a monster. At first she refused to come out of her room, even to meet the guy. That rude act embarrassed her mother terribly.

Finally on the third date Melanie crept out of her bedroom, grunted hello to the bewildered man and plopped herself on the nearest chair. Sternly she folded her arms, crossed her legs, and glared at the wall.

"How are things at school?" the man asked awkwardly.

"Just great," Melanie moaned. She then reached quickly for the television remote and turned on the set. Just as rapidly she crawled up the volume to an irritating pitch.

"Mrs. Toonly said she would check in on you." Her mother's anger was starting to boil. "You have her number if you need anything."

"Oh, sure," Melanie growled. "Don't worry about old Melanie. I'll just eat the chips and clean out the cookies." Click, click, click, she raced across the channels.

Finally her mother and her date left with frowns of bewilderment on their faces. What was happening, they wondered. How could an otherwise delightful person turn into a monster whenever her mother went out with a man? Certainly the date hadn't done anything; Melanie saw to it that they didn't even get close to each other.

At age eleven Melanie was a bit old to throw a tantrum. But somehow her personality went through a radical change whenever date-night came.

Someone needs to sit down with Melanie and ask her some serious questions. Maybe she isn't fully aware of what is going on. A few questions to start with would be:

- Are you afraid of losing your mother?
- Do you want all of her attention?
- Are you still dreaming of getting your father back?
- Is there something that frightens you about this person?
- Is there something about being left alone at night that bothers you?
- Are you afraid of getting a new father?
- Are you afraid a new parent will mean you might move?
- Is there someone else you want your mother to date?

There is a reason why a person becomes a monster, even if for a little while. A few good questions and answers could help children like Melanie become themselves again.

◆ ◆ ◆ ◆ ◆

Home Alone

With so many parents working outside the home, millions of children are left alone. They might be alone for an hour or two every day—sometimes longer.

Some children like being left alone and others don't. It depends on the child, how long they are alone, what the circumstances are, and how old the child is. What works for one child may not be good for another.

If you are being left alone and you don't like it, your parent needs to know that. Too many children are afraid to be alone and don't say anything. Don't be afraid to upset or disappoint your parent. You shouldn't pretend and tell your parent it's all right when it really isn't.

If you feel uncomfortable being alone, you need to tell your parent. Tell her exactly why it bothers you. Describe the problem so she will understand and ask questions. Brainstorm some possible solutions together. Parents usually can help if they know how you feel.

Often your parent can make an adjustment or two and you might feel better about being home alone. Let your parent in on the problem. Don't simply hide your feelings because you don't want to bother your parent. You are there to help each other. Maybe you can work together to improve your situation.

Bake a Cake—
Make a Model

What do you do when you have only one parent? If you want to, you can sit in the living room and silently watch reruns—your parent sitting in an overstuffed chair and you sprawled out on the couch.

There the two of you sit for hours. You don't talk much. You watch a black-and-white situation comedy from the 1960s. Life sure is boring living with one parent and doing nothing on a dull evening.

Get up! Get moving! Get thinking! Get creating! Have fun together!

Go outside and race down the street to the store. Take a ball to the park and get active. Order a pizza and have an anchovies fight. Don't sit around the house like a couple of cushions.

Break out the flour and bake something tasty. Invent a new food that never has been eaten. Buy a cheap model and put it together. Any old car or boat or plane will do. Pick up a puzzle at a garage sale and put it together. Borrow some good books from the library to read together. If you just sit around all the time, the circulation in your legs may stop and your toes may turn orange.

Single parents aren't beanbag chairs. They have life. They're real. Teach yourself how to skateboard or sing rap. See if your parent knows how to do the chicken walk.

Get up! Get moving! Get thinking! Get creating! Have fun together!

◆ ◆ ◆ ◆ ◆

Loneliness Is a Choice

On a Friday night, Sean sat home alone playing Nintendo. His dad sat in one room watching television and Sean stayed in his room, by himself.

The clock ticked slowly on his dresser. A digital clock flashed green numbers on the nightstand. Mindlessly, Sean aimed the car down the middle of the road, and blew it up.

As a sixth grader, Sean didn't like being alone on a Friday night. He was bored, and being bored made him think he was a dork.

Before long he felt sorry for himself. "If only I had a large family," Sean thought. "With brothers and sisters running everywhere, I wouldn't have to be alone." Soon he was dreary and depressed.

It's easy to get the lonely blues when you sit by yourself all evening. Being alone is good now and then. Being alone too much is a real bummer.

In Sean's case, his dad was in the next room. Friends were only as far away as his phone. There were half a dozen people who would enjoy hearing from him. They could come over or he could go over to their place.

Sean was making choices. He wanted to spend time with other people, but he refused to make the effort to make a contact.

Most of us do that. We get upset at ourselves for not getting together with others. Yet we sit around like paint drying and do nothing about it.

No one is likely to drive up to our door with a truckload of musicians and try to cheer us up. We can't wait for the Russian Ballet to hurry over and entertain us. We need to make a decision and move toward people. Maybe we don't have money or the "right clothes," but we have gifts to share—jokes, stories, a dance move, artistic talent, or whatever it is.

People of all ages find themselves bored and stuck with nothing to do. Sometimes we try to connect with a friend and aren't able to. But most of the time if we reach out we will find someone who is looking for something to do.

If you are lonely it probably isn't because you only have one parent. Usually we are lonely because we don't go to the trouble to contact someone. We may feel nervous at first, but it will get easier with practice.

❖ ❖ ❖ ❖ ❖

Too Old for Baby-Sitters

How do you feel when your parent wants to go out for an evening or away for a Saturday and he gets someone to come over and watch you? Are you happy, or do you think you are too old to have a baby-sitter?

The problem really gets sticky if you have younger brothers and sisters who definitely need a baby-sitter, but your parent doesn't want you to baby-sit them. Do you get a thirteen-year-old baby-sitter when you are 10½? It's hard to figure out sometimes.

Let's come at this problem from a different angle. The most important question is not whether or not you need a baby-sitter. You might have a great day alone. The more important question is does your parent need for you to have a baby-sitter?

If your parent cannot go out and have peace of mind, then you need a baby-sitter. You can't expect your parent to worry all evening about how you are doing. If he is going to be nervous all evening, he might as well stay home.

Parents and children have to think about each other. It can't always be what is best for the child. A parent's comfort level is a high priority. When a parent is nervous or rattled, the children often feel upset, too.

Welcome the baby-sitter, no matter how old he might be. Have fun! Watch television together and raid the refrigerator. You will be doing your parent a big favor. That's important.

◆ ◆ ◆ ◆ ◆

Growing up Fast

Kristy didn't have many responsibilities around the house. She came home from school, grabbed a pack of cookies and a glass of milk, and headed for the television set. From 4:00 to 6:00 she ate, watched "Jeanie Gets a Broken Heart," and vegetated on the couch.

At 6:00 the family hurried and ate supper and soon Kristy was back in television land. During the evening she fielded phone calls from friends and filed her nails.

A good person, Kristy was slow at growing up. Her home life wasn't very challenging and she didn't learn much. Some evenings her biggest decision was whether to eat the entire cookie with one bite or separate the pieces and lick the filling out.

Across the street we find Anthony. Every evening he was expected to care for a younger brother and younger sister, do the family laundry, and start fixing supper at 5:45 on the dot. Seldom did Anthony have time to himself; he continually carried responsibilities for others.

There was no time for Anthony to be a child. He was growing up so fast that his childhood was whizzing past him. Later, when Anthony becomes an adult, he will probably look back and wonder how he missed being young.

Kristy's life sounds like fun if you want to grow up to look like a cookie. At her present pace she will grow up very slowly and could find it tough to handle responsibilities.

Anthony's world of work looks too demanding. Certainly he needs to help around the house, but when does this boy have time to be a kid? Is he going to become an eleven-year-old adult and never play ball?

Parents and children need to talk. They need to decide how fast a child should grow up; how many responsibilities they should have; how much fun, play, creative, and explorative time they should enjoy. There ought to be a steady growth. The best pattern is to accept more and more responsibilities as one grows older while keeping plenty of creative time too.

Often a child in a single parent home, especially an older child, will try hard to help out. They see so much to do and they want to help their stressed-out parent. That's a great idea. All families should pull together to get everything done. But smart kids will be part grown up and part young. And a thinking parent will make sure his child gets a balance.

If you find yourself constantly worrying about everyone else and trying to do everything, you need to slow down. Life is often difficult, but don't forget to be a child.

"Jesus said, 'Let the little children come to me, and do not hinder them, for the kingdom of heaven belongs to such as these'" (Matthew 19:14).

Pitching In

Amy was complaining because she had so much work to do around the house. Her single mother expected Amy to vacuum the hall regularly and help with the dishes. Two nights a week, Tuesday and Thursday, Amy was expected to start supper. Eleven years old, Amy thought she was overworked and it wasn't fair. Her friends with two parents didn't have to do so much work, she insisted. They got to go out more and have fun. Amy pouted.

When things didn't go the way Amy wanted them to go, she had a habit of blaming everything on her situation. To hear her tell it, all of Amy's problems would be solved if she only had both parents around.

Amy didn't want to accept the fact that all children should help around the house. Whether they have a single parent or not, children need to pitch in and share some of the responsibilities at home.

Children can dust, pick up papers, water plants, make beds, take care of pets, iron clothes, and a great many other jobs. The reason children should help is that they live there. They aren't guests at a hotel with maids and butlers. They aren't kings or queens, and their parents aren't servants waiting on them.

Household jobs can make everyone feel better about themselves. By pitching in we know we are an important part of the family. We also learn to take care of ourselves as we grow up.

Children who can do their own laundry, make their own appointments, and cook some meals often feel more confident about themselves. Pitching in is good experience and a great way to show a solid love for each other.

Are some children overworked at home by their parents as Amy seems to suggest? No doubt some children are, but not very many. Most children watch television for hours when they could lend a helping hand. Fifteen minutes of pitching in would make a big difference.

Instead of helping, some children would rather whine. The minute their parent gives them a job, they start to complain as though they were going to die at any minute. If a parent is smart, she will make the child carry out the job in spite of the noisemaking. If the child has any sense, she will get at the job and get it done. Some children spend more time and energy trying to get out of a job than they would use getting the job done.

Do the children of single parents have to work harder around the house? Maybe. Maybe not. But if they help, they can make life far more enjoyable.

◆ ◆ ◆ ◆ ◆

Expensive Athletic Shoes

When Matt walked through the mall he was hypnotized by athletic shoes. Keeping his eyes low, the fifth grader checked out feet as he poked along the hall. Matt noticed how new the shoes were and he always looked for the brand names. He was impressed with that kind of thing.

Not that Matt was walking around barefoot. He had a good pair of athletic shoes. They weren't exactly new, but they weren't worn out either.

Matt's shoes bothered him. To begin with they didn't have a famous brand name. They weren't the kind that basketball stars wore and advertised on television. Matt didn't feel cool wearing shoes that no one had heard of.

Besides, Matt's mother took him to a discount shoe store to buy them. He was totally bummed out about that. What if his friends saw him getting plain shoes in a cheap store? Worse than that, what if some of the big shots from school saw him going into the store? Matt felt embarrassed about the whole mess.

Matt was almost always self-conscious about his shoes. He scuffed dirt on them so they wouldn't look too new. He didn't want his friends reading that odd-ball brand name on them.

If you happened to notice when Matt sat around with people his age, he almost always pulled his feet back under his chair or bench. He didn't want anyone to see what he was wearing.

Clothes are important to most of us. We may not need the latest fashion in everything but we don't want to look too strange either. Clothes are like our hair and skin. People see our clothes first and we want them to think well of us.

Most of us want normal, average clothes with good enough shoes so we won't look odd or weird. We want to get looked at but not stared at.

Sometimes we act like Matt. Our hopes become fixed on a jacket, or a hat, or a shirt, and if we don't get it we are simply "going to die." We think our whole life is going to crumble if we can't get that set of threads.

If we calm down and think about what's important, we know that athletic shoes and Girbaud jeans aren't really what counts. Beauty is only skin deep. The important parts of a person are kindness, love, friendship, helpfulness, thoughtfulness, and things like that.

Let's pretend for a minute that you know Matt. One day, sitting alone at a lunch table, Matt tells you that he can't stand it because he can't have a pair of expensive athletic shoes. If Matt told you that, what would you say?

"Do not consider his appearance or his height. . . . The LORD does not look at the things man looks at. Man looks at the outward appearance, but the LORD looks at the heart" (1 Samuel 16:7).

◆ ◆ ◆ ◆ ◆

Without Discipline!

Doesn't discipline sound terrible? Discipline sounds mean and harsh. Sometimes we think a parent must be awful if he disciplines the children.

Let's pretend that you had a child and never disciplined the kid. How would your child behave?

He might throw food at meal time.
She might chew on the electrical wires.
He could plug up the sink and let the water overflow onto the floor.

Soon it would become clear that your child needs discipline. Otherwise he or she will wreck the house and get hurt. Discipline can be a great idea.

But you're no little baby. Do you need discipline at your age? Let's pretend again.

Suppose you stacked grilled cheese sandwiches under your bed for weeks and attracted ants and mice.
Suppose you made calls all day and ran up the telephone bill.
Suppose you beat up your younger brother or sister.

If you did things like that, you would need discipline. Someone would need to say "No, you can't do that."

That's what discipline is: someone draws a line and says you can't go beyond that. If discipline is done correctly it helps protect a person. Good discipline is not designed to hurt people but to help them. It is like a safety net. Discipline and punishment are not the same thing.

Most children don't enjoy discipline but they also know there is a good purpose for it. Sometimes we are glad that our parents stopped us from doing something dumb.

Many children are in a hurry to run their own lives and make their own decisions. That sounds great. We should discipline ourselves. But if we don't set limits ourselves, we need a parent or someone else to enforce limits for us.

A parent who loves you will discipline you. He can't be cruel or abusive; that isn't love. But a loving parent will stop you from doing some things.

Sometimes your parents will discipline you and you might want to say, "You don't love me." You will get over that feeling. Often we know that our parent really does love us.

Discipline, done right, is a sign of love.

"Discipline your children while there is hope" (Proverbs 19:18 NRSV).

◆ ◆ ◆ ◆ ◆

Your Parent-Friend

Living with one parent brought many changes to Megan's world. She spent a lot of time close to her mother and they shared experiences. Twelve-year-old Megan talked about her sixth grade teacher and Mother told her about the neat guy she met at work.

Megan enjoyed their relationship. She began to think of her mother as more of an older friend than a parent. They went shopping together and stopped for hot chocolate at the donut shop. Megan felt grown up and liked being on a level with her mother.

One night Megan picked up an armful of tapes, slung her coat over her shoulder, and said, "I'm going to Sarah's; I'll be home by midnight."

"You'll be home when?" her mother sounded shocked.

"I said by midnight; no big deal."

"It's a school night, young lady. You'll be home by ten."

"I think I'm old enough to decide what time I need to be home," Megan said angrily.

"And I think I'm still your mother. Midnight's too late for a school girl."

Megan's closeness to her mother had become confusing. The sixth grader started to think she was older than she really was. She began to believe she was an equal to her mother rather than still a child.

Understandably, Megan was maturing quickly. She was taking on more responsibility and more decision making. Her mother gave her credit for doing so many things well.

Unfortunately in the rush Megan forgot that a single parent is still a parent. As a parent her mother has to remain in charge as long as Megan is a child.

For many years there will be some decisions about which a parent must have the final say. Though she turns over more decision making to her children, the single parent, like other parents, remains the authority in a child's life.

A single parent doesn't mean there is no parent or only half a parent. A single parent is a full and total parent all of a child's growing up years.

It may not be a child's fault if she gets confused. The single parent may have given the child a tremendous amount of freedom. The child may run a great deal of her own life. Eventually the child could start to feel in charge.

The Bible gives us some guidelines for parent and child relationships. These instructions apply whether we have two parents in residence or one.

For instance the Bible tells us to obey our parents. Every family needs to operate on that principle. As long as you are at home growing up, your parent has the final word.

"Children, obey your parents in the Lord, for this is right"(Ephesians 6:1).

Private Eye

Have you ever wanted to be a real-life private detective? How would you like to collect clues, follow people, and sneak around corners to see who is up to what? Would it be fun to find evidence and report back to headquarters?

The work of a private eye looks exciting on television and maybe you will want to be one when you grow up. But doing detective work in our family is likely to get us in trouble and hurt someone's feelings.

Imagine that your father who doesn't live with you asks you to do some detective work. He wants you to keep your eye open and tell him what kind of men your mother dates. That sounds easy. You can picture yourself listening through the wall at night or hiding behind the couch. Later you can see yourself reporting each bit of evidence to your father.

Or suppose your mother's boyfriend wants to know if she has any other male friends. Or what if your mother wants a full report of what goes on at your father's house? What if mother asks you to find out how much money your father makes?

Sometimes grandparents want to know everything that's going on. They might ask what time mother comes home from dates or whom she talks to on the phone.

Maybe that sounds exciting. Piecing together a case from traces of information is a great challenge. But children shouldn't be used as detectives to investigate their own families. When adult relatives ask a child to snoop and report back, they put that child in a tough situation. They are asking that child to betray someone he loves.

There is a place for real detective work but that's for adults. No one should ask you to collect clues in your own family. That's one adult trying to use a child in order to hurt another adult. Adults should not use children for this.

If you agree to do detective work, you may soon find that no one trusts you. Your parents and friends will stop talking around you because they are afraid you will report on them.

Families are founded on trust and love and a certain amount of acceptance. If we think that one family member is a detective, we will close up and stop sharing.

If an adult asks you to "keep an eye" on a family member and report what you see, tell that person, "I don't play detective with my own family." That way you won't cause trouble by poking for clues and you can maintain a loving, trusting relationship with both adults.

Parents at Big Events

What are some of the big events that parents usually attend? Frequently we see parents at:

school plays and musical performances
church programs and concerts
piano recitals
sporting events
confirmation ceremonies
parent-teacher conferences
camp programs

These are important times in a child's life and usually parents like to attend if they are able. But when children live with one parent, the other parent often presents a problem.

If the absent parent is in the military or in a hospital or in prison, the situation can be handled easily. The parent at home may want to send a copy of the program and a photo to share with the parent who couldn't attend. You might even want to send a note to describe the occasion.

A different problem is when the parent at home and the other parent don't get along well.

91

They may both be able to attend the event but they don't want to sit together.

If your parents don't care to sit together at one of your events, that's their decision to make. You may have trouble understanding the ill feelings between your parents, but your parents have a right to feel however they think they have to feel. You shouldn't try to change your parents' attitudes.

If you want both parents at a special event, speak up! Don't let them guess whether or not you want them there. Call, write, do whatever it takes. Let each parent know that you want both of them sitting there watching.

Don't be surprised or deeply hurt if they both can't make it. Almost certainly you will have friends there who have only one parent in attendance. One parent is enjoyable, too, as you have probably learned before.

There are all kinds of family combinations in this world. Simply try to enjoy the mix of parents you have. If you have two parents in the area and you want both of them at your special event, say something to each of them individually. That's one way to keep your relationship with both parents alive and growing.

◆ ◆ ◆ ◆ ◆

What Do You Think?

There was a boy who lived in Baltimore and everyone told him what to think.

Teachers told him what to learn.
Parents told him what to do.
Ministers told him what to believe.

But no one asked the boy in Baltimore what he thought.

The boy had friends who told him what they knew.

Kevin told him about frogs.
Jenny told him about books.
Lenny told him about video games.

But none of his friends ever asked him what he thought.

The boy from Baltimore joined a club.

They showed him how to tie ropes.
They showed him how to take hikes.
They showed him how to shoot a rifle.

But no one in the group ever asked him what he thought.

One day, sitting at the kitchen table with his mother, he heard his mother say,

"Son, what do you think?"
"What?" The boy was startled.
"You know," she continued, "about going on a picnic with your stepbrothers. What do you think?"

The boy from Baltimore was pleased because someone asked, "What do you think?"

Can't Take Their Place

If you ever lose a hand, you will never get another one like it. Your parent may buy another hand that looks like the first one but it will never be the same.

The new hand will be made of plastic, rubber, or some new material. It will run on wires and maybe even batteries. The replacement hand will look good and do a lot of neat things. But the new hand can never be the hand you used to have.

Suppose your father or mother no longer lives with you. Your single parent might marry again someday, but your new parent can never be exactly like your first parent.

No one can be the same as your original parent. No adult friends, no uncles or aunts, no grandparents, no neighbor—no one can be the parent you once had.

Some children have a parent who has died. Others have a parent who is in prison, or a parent who has run away and never returned. Often a child will hope to get a new parent just like the one who is gone.

That's asking too much. No one can take your parent's place. Someone might become your stepfather or stepmother but even they won't be the same as the parent who was first.

That's good news! No one will ever become your original parent. If your parent has died, you can still love him as you did when he was alive. You don't have to feel guilty because you love your new parent. It's okay to love both of them. Your first dad and your stepdad are different, and it's possible to love both of them.

You can enjoy your new hand even if it will never be the same as your first hand.

Some children get confused because they think they have to make a choice. Should they love one or the other? It's possible to love them both.

You can love two or three sets of grandparents. No one says you have to choose between them. You can love three or four sisters or brothers all at once. Who would say you have to stop loving a brother before you can love a sister?

God gave us a tremendous ability to love. You can love a dozen relatives all at one time. You don't have to love one person less so you can begin loving another relative.

The memory you have of a parent can always be precious. Thank God for that parent.

"I thank my God every time I remember you" (Philippians 1:3).